AF440980

I SAID I WOULD FOLLOW YOU ANYWHERE, BUT A LIGHTHOUSE? WHERE'S THE TOWN?

By

Sandy Black

515 South Flower Street, 18th and 19th Floors,

Los Angeles, California, 90071

ISBN: 978-1-83663-006-7

Library of Congress Number: 2022915634

You may visit her at her website: booksbysandyllc.com

and email: blackbrunson5@gmail.com

This book is a work of fiction. Names, characters, places are a

product of the authors imagination.

Table of Contents

Dedication:

To each person who throughout lighthouse history made safety at sea a priority.

Acknowledgement:

To Kristin

Her love of lighthouses gave me the energy to complete this book

Chapter One

The Stowaways

It was a blustery day in 1858. 'Kitty Kolza' was patiently waiting on Miss Nelly to finish cleaning and polishing the new heavier window that was just installed. Replacing new windows, among many other things, seems to be a normal day in the dilapidated old lighthouse building. She decided it was too early to meander down to the beach. Low tide was not until later, so napping in the central brick tower Keepers dwelling made a lot of sense. Today, like most days, the storms would come and go. Raging and calming and taking their toll. Right now nothing is happening on the small islet, which is connected to the shore by an isthmus and only accessible at low tides.

'Lighty' watched 'Kitty Kolza' as she made her way to the Keepers quarters.

"Hi, 'Kitty Kolza', my keepers sure are keeping busy. Before they arrived, it was being considered to tear me down and start over. At least the part that was destroyed by continued ocean battering. I was really nervous. But, thankfully, the Jeffries, a dedicated couple, little by little are making changes and I continue to look better each year. And my lamps continue to glow. Best of all, my constant companion keeps a smile on all our faces. I'm sure glad you are here, 'Kitty Kolza'."

'Kitty Kolza' said, "Oh! Me too. I was rescued off one of the small ships from which many did not make to shore. I kinda wish we had other family and friends here, don't you?" 'Kitty Kolza' looked across the ocean where there was intermittent fog, a lot of wind storms and dangerous beaches as far as the eye could see. Her mother was lost at sea, and seeing the approaching fog made her homesick. There is always a chance of another foundering ship that fills with water, sinks or runs aground. Back to napping.

Awakened from her nap, 'Kitty Kolza' thought it was her melancholy feeling, but something just did not feel right. The Keepers were talking about a huge storm, and although the fourth-order Fresnel lens in the lantern room produced enough light from the Colza oil to be spotted by ships fourteen miles out, the dim light from a ship seen earlier had disappeared. This could mean that it was safely on its way to a destination or it had capsized with no survivors. This happened far too often. The reef is not at all forgiving. "Lighty, do you know I was named after the oil made from the wild cabbage called Colza, which my Master's family grew on the farm? Mother named me 'Kitty Kolza' because I was born near the Colza presses. We, like many slaves, stowed away on ships headed to a better life. Many perished, including my mother and her Master."

"'Lighty, Lighty, do something!" 'Kitty Kolza' screeched. "Turn the lantern up! Something is floating in the water! Help!!" Mr. John and Mrs. Nellie grabbed rain cover and went running down the path as quickly as they could. It was hard to keep the lanterns lit due to the thrashing waves. 'Kitty Kolza', along with her keepers, saw a tiny boat that appeared to be covered with a heavy canvas. Thinking it to be salvage cargo from a merchant ship, they pulled it up and over the rocks and sand. All of a sudden, Mrs. Nellie yelled, "What is that noise? It sounds like puppies! Get that top off!" Three little baskets, all wrapped in water-resistant material. The first was a little dog whimpering and shaking. The second basket, 'Kitty Kolza', thinking it another puppy, jumped back a said, "What is that? Why, it's a little white duck. She cuddled up against the little dog while the couple pulled the top off the third basket. Mrs. Nellie looked down, and there was a tiny, rosy-cheeked baby girl. "Oh, John, they survived. Look, pinned to the baby's blanket is a note."

The note read:

"If you should find my little family, and they are alive, would you see they are raised in a Christian home. Mary Catherine McSavy, Dexter and Doodles, the duck who does not quack. He thinks he is a dog. We are stowaways, and no one will know to even miss us. May God richly bless you for their care.

That night, when all were safe in the warmth of the Battery Point Lighthouse, 'Kitty Kolza' said, " 'Lighty', how lucky we are that our keepers decided to stay, and look, we now have new additions to our family. With lots of tender loving care, we can all survive the storm. Lighty smiled, "Yup, we have withstood it all. You name it, we have weathered all kinds of storms, and I mean all kinds. I have a newly painted tower, and the Keepers quarters are liveable again. I also heard something else. The keepers are thinking they will start a family soon."

"Well, it looks to me like we have a good start already. Now, if we can teach that duck how to quack. Barking like a dog is just not right." 'Kitty Kolza' laughed and cuddled up near Mrs. Nellie in an old family rocker with Mary Catherine. Everyone gave thanks and smiled.

Lighty thought he heard a faint quack.

Chapter Two
The Little Lighthouse That Loved Railroads - of the Underground Kind

"Lake Erie is so dark. It seems as though the sun has lost its way and never finds us", frowned 'Kitty Ash'. "Along with stormy nights, sudden out-of-nowhere gales, mist and fog, one wonders how our little town Ashtabula on the Ohio River still stands. The little lighthouse looked down at his coal-black, furry ball of feline cuteness and said, "Sort of reminds me, before my time, of when the British and Americans fought with at least five Indian tribes for the Great Lakes. Finally, I'm told between the signing of The Treaty of Greenville and the Rush-Baget Agreement, which limited military vessals in the waters, we finally have no more maritime battles. However, bad storms and vessel explosions didn't stop the fast-growing trade business, which caused a lot of loss of life. Not to mention all the diseases like smallpox and typhoid, and other secret events. You know, I actually came about because all the other Harbors had beacon lights except Ashtabul. I was built for $2,000 with the help of the local merchants, and now we can see it across the Province of Ontario, Canada. *And that's not all my story, but what about you, 'Kitty Ash'?"*

"I actually came up the Ohio River with my slave family, the Orsens. You see, we are part of the Underground Railroad. Most of us who came this way were from Kentucky. We came through the caves and then across the river into Indiana. Me and my dear friend, 'Kitty Ossie' were what is called 'Woods Guides'. We took people through the caves and watched out for those nasty slave hunters. We made it all the way to Ashtabula, which is the end of the Underground Railroad, before sailing to Ontario, Canada. By the end, I mean it is the last stop to freedom. We have been part of a network of abolitionist families who help transport slave families like mine into fourteen free states and, in our case, on to the Providence of Ontario, Canada. We were called 'freight' (slaves) and were assigned a Conductor. His job is to get us safely all the way to freedom. One of the houses I stayed in was 'Mother Hubbard Cupboard'. She had six children, and no one ever suspected her as a person who worked full-time to provide food, clothing, and shelter for slaves escaping from the South. She had a trap door in the kitchen that led to a secret cellar under the kitchen where we hid the slaves. There was an octagon-shaped house high on the hill that served as a lookout for slave catchers. My dearly loved slave, Mr. Orson, was searching for his wife and children, who had been sold to a slave master. In his search for them, he trusted the wrong people and lost his life after a snitch, who wanted to make a quick buck, turned him in. He was beaten and branded. Our slave family felt he just gave up and died. He hid me and 'Kitty Ossie' on one of those farmers' wagons that the Quakers used to help move us, and I ended up here. If I had not found you, I would no doubt be staying at Mother Hubbards." 'Kitty Ash' looked across the water and said softly, "I believe I was saved for a reason. Not to go to Canada but to continue to guide slaves from house to house here. To make sure they are safely on whatever water vessel they can get on to freedom. That's my story."

The little lighthouse, 'Kitty Ash' affectionately called 'Fisky', looked through tears and said, "It seems we both share a secret. I love the work of the Underground Railroad and the people who help the slaves on their final sail to freedom and Ontario, Canada. I need you to know about the Hiram Lake House. Those who stop there to get on a ship, the Conductor sends me a signal. Then I turn my lights on so they can quietly slip out of the harbor. I am so happy you were saved, and we can now openly work together to save many more lives. Someday, we will retire when all slaves are free. Until then, you will have a permanent pillow with your friend in the Keepers quarters.

"Thanks 'Fisky', and where might that pillow be about right now? 'Fisky' was about as happy as a little lighthouse could be. "Good night 'Kitty Ash'."

Chapter Three
Tiny Harbor, Shipwrecks Galore - Somebody Do Something!

"Well, I've heard of round barns, but not some 8-sided thing called octagon", a baffled 'Kitty Oscar' said to his friend, 'Kitty Knicker'. "Just more gossip, I guess", responded 'Kitty Knicker'. "I've been around a long while here, and when I heard a rumble that all of the merchants were up in arms because two of every four ships that approach the lower New York Harbor, too often are caught up in our unseen sand bars and shoals that are so treacherous. They end up crashing and losing so much money in lost cargo. It is causing severe hardships!" 'Kitty Oscar' said, "That must be why everybody was up gathering and talking in the square about the merchants petitioning the Colonial Assembly to get a lighthouse built. It could help guide ships safely through the Harbor."

'Kitty Knicker' said when she was down on the dock, 'Kitty Ebony' and 'Kitty Marconi, the big yard bosses, told several of the locals that Mr.& Mrs. Hartshorne, the owners of a place called Sandy Hook, sold four acres of that land for a lighthouse. They had been thinking it was doubtful they could ever sell it, but they did - for 750 pounds." "Good gosh, 'Kitty Knicker', you and I both know those boys don't always tell the truth. They make things up to look like they know everything." He emphatically replied, "I know, I know, but I was told on good authority that the assembly passed "an act for raising a sum of money not to exceed three thousand pounds by way of a lottery for building a lighthouse." 'Kitty Oscar' raised his eyebrows and said, "And you believe that?" "Well, 'Kitty Marconi' came from those high-ups in the Marconi family. In fact, it is believed that he is from a rare bloodline of feline dignitaries dating back to companions to the King of England! He knows stuff." 'Kitty Oscar' rolled over laughing. *"and, I came from the Oscar McNutt family off the good ship, 'Dreamer', and I will believe it when I see it."*

Three Years Later

Barren, sandy soil suddenly began to grow to 103 feet and nine stories high. Each day 'Kitty Oscar' sat down next to his three friends to watch the progress. They marveled each day how that octagon-shaped-looking building was growing and taking shape into a real lighthouse with a seven-foot high Lantern House. "This will soon be our home. All of us will be making sure the lighthouse is safe for the new Keepers. 'Kitty Oscar' said, I will be in charge of the upper level. The entire lower part and grounds will keep you guys busy since those darn skunks love lighthouses, as do other critters. The Lantern House is made of iron, and our roof is copper, and don't forget, the forty-eight oil blazes which should make our jobs easier."

"Good grief, an Armada could see us!" said 'Kitty Ebony', who usually said very little. We will never be known as a little cove anymore. The merchants are elated, and so are we. It feels good not to have so many crashed ships, pulling shipmen out of the water, and to finally see everyone make it safely into the Harbor."

"I told you 'Kitty Marconi' came from Royalty and is brilliant. He knew we were going to have a lighthouse. Just brilliant!" said 'Kitty Knicker'. "Oh, stop it. He'll want a crown next!" giggled 'Kitty Oscar'. What do you guys think of a name for her? 'Kitty Marconi' said, "What about Queen Darby - you know, royal and all?" "Or Sandylot." "Those are silly,"....chimed in the others. 'Kitty Oscar' thought a minute. "Why not just call her The Sandy Hook Lighthouse?"

June, 1764. The Sandy Hook Lighthouse was lit for the first time.

Chapter Four
Looks More Like a Glowworm Than a
Lighthouse Beacon!

'Kitty Isere' stood on top of the highest flat rock she could find. 'Kittys Kory, Kilee and Kora', the British short hair triplets in their fluffy, British blue coats were watching for a hi-sign from their friend, 'Kitty Isere', to come to their viewing place. 'Kitty Isere' was wearing a French flag scarf around her neck and shouted down to her friends to hurry up and get to their perch. Today was an extraordinary day. The Statue of Liberty Enlightening the World copper sculpture, a gift from France, was to arrive on Liberty Island in New York Harbor today.

"I told you to arrive early! I could have given your spots away five times! This is my day! You should know, I am a French royal! , shouted 'Kitty Isere'. In fact, I was named after the French Steamer Isere'." 'Kitty Kory' said, "You are a royal alright - a royal pain in my neck! You dragged us out here through 200,000 people to see a big head that some French dude made with no place to stand her up! Really!"

"You don't understand. Listen up! My mother was the prized French feline companion, 'Kitty Rene' Renoit' to Edouard Rene' de Laboulaye's wife. When they visited the United States to support the Union during the Civil War, and during the time when the war ended, and the abolition of slavery took place, 'Kitty Renoit' fell in love with my father, 'Kitty Bartholdi'. His master, Frederic Bartholdi, was the French sculptor who designed the copper statue gift given to the United States from France. My mother went back to France with Mrs. de Laboulage to help in the movement for democracy in her own country and find solutions for their anti-slavery issues similar to those experienced in the United States. We lived in the Bartholdi sculptor's studio until my father passed. I have been on my own ever since looking for a new Forever Home, and I think I have found it."

"Wow, what a story. Now I understand the scarf, said 'Kitty Kilee'. "I did hear the French were going to pay for her head, and *what a head she has,* and the United States will pay for her pedestal."

"And here we are. July 17, 1885. Yup, here she comes right through the Harbor to her final home. This is so exciting. She is going to be a statue and a lighthouse." 'Kitty Isere' stood on her two hind feet. Tall, proud and smiling.

'Kitty Kory', being her usual argumentative self, spoke over the noise of the excited crowd, "OK, now let me play the Devil's advocate here. How on earth do you expect a statue/lighthouse to function as a lighthouse? Where are all those fancy engineer brains? We are landlocked from all sides. Manhattan, Continental US, Brooklyn and New Jersey. We can't even be seen from the ocean. A lighthouse is supposed to guide ships in or caution them to stop so they can avoid a shipwreck." 'Kitty Kory' chimed in, "And how you gonna light that big thing up?"

"Good questions, said 'Kitty Isere'. I heard The American Electric Light Manufacturing Company is moving to the Island, and the lighthouse will be electric. Even pay for it..you know, all that new fangled stuff." "I sure hope somebody knows what they are doing 'cause that torch thing in her hand is going to be 305 feet 'way up there,'." cackled 'Kitty Kilee'.

October, 1886

President Cleveland had closely watched the assembling of the Statue of Liberty Lighthouse and, upon its completion, declared it to be under the auspices of the United States Lighthouse Board and officially a lighthouse. 'Kitty Isire' announced she would be moving into the lighthouse with the first Head Keeper, Albert E. Littlefield. "He has specialization in electricity knowledge! she told her friends. I wish my mother and father were here to see this magnificent statue."

Over time, the beautiful copper Statue of Liberty/Lighthouse was finding it difficult to be a working lighthouse. Even on the night of the dedication, 'Kitty Isere', along with her 'fluffy friends' witnesses, there was only a faint gleam. It was barely visible from Manhattan. No floodlights on the balcony of the torch. "A big OOPS", said 'Kitty Kilee'. They were denied clearance for the lights because they might blind ship pilots as they passed by the statue." "Good grief, said 'Kitty Kory'. We could get better light from our six orange eyes shining at night than that glowworm thing."

Sixteen Years Later

The lighthouse continues to serve. However, she has a 'Keeper of the Flame', who is responsible for making sure the light bulb does not burn out. Who would have thot'!

The four feline best friends agreed, "She may not be a good aid to navigate ships, but she sure has become a landmark that defines the New York City skyline. The first thing a new immigrant sees coming to the United States is a beautiful, proud woman standing on a large pedestal with her right arm extended holding high a flaming torch. A turreted crown with huge spikes symbolizing the rays of the sun rests on her head. At her feet, a broken shackle symbolizes the overthrow of tyranny. She weighs in at 100 tons and 151 feet tall." What a majestic feat! All agreed.

The Statue of Liberty is more than a lighthouse. She is THE Symbol of the promise of America.

Chapter Five

Between Seeing Double and Dozens of 'Firsts', I'm getting Dizzy!

"We could use some help down here!"

"All those horrid storms and dangerous currents that navigators of ships coming down the Atlantic coast talk endlessly about are taking a huge toll on life. Having no light at night to guide them is most certainly going to lead to more disasters, shouted 'Kitty Horatio' to his twin sister, 'Kitty Holly'. "I'm tired of us being part of a non-stop clean-up crew."

'Kitty Horatio' continued to grumble, "You would think being part of the Highlands that overlook the entrance to New York Bay and the hills that we are told are the highest points along the eastern seaboard, someone would figure it out." "OK, OK. I told you a while back that big changes are coming. I am told we are going to have a new Lighthouse. If you would complain less and listen to the human conversations all around us, you would hear we are in for some monumental moves and many 'firsts'. So be patient, my brother."

"Is that thing going to be a lighthouse or a fortress for war? Did that guy, Nimrod Woodward, know that the land he sold for $600 was going to be a castle-like fortress-looking structure? TWO towers!! One tower is octagonal at one end, and the other is square at the opposite end. What was someone drinkin' when they decided to build twin lighthouses with twin lights linked to each other with Keepers quarters? We will be living, by the way?" They are not even identical twin towers," growled 'Kitty Horatio'. "So, we are non-identical twins. What's your point!" said his sister, who was getting aggravated with her twin brother, who clearly did not like change. He was perfectly okay with living in an old dilapidated lighthouse.

"I see so many wonderful 'firsts' in our soon-to-be Navasink - Two Tower Lighthouse. We are going to be 64 feet high atop a 200 ft hill overlooking the Shrewsbury River. And with our two beacons - one fixed and the other that flashes, we now will be able to see the ships at night." "You do give a convincing argument," said 'Kitty Horatio'. I need a nap."

Sometime later- the 1862 rebuild

'Kitty Holly' asked her twin brother to join her in the Keeper quarters. There was going to be a meeting where some inspectors were coming to inspect the lighthouse. Congress had paid big bucks to have her built. "Shhh," said 'Kitty Holly'. I love being part of all these 'firsts,' don't you? Why, I'm hearing them say, we are the first lighthouse to have twin towers, first to have two beacons, first to test the revolutionary Fresnel lens design and first to have two beehive-shaped lights. And that's not all. We are going to have Guglielmo Marconi come and do a demonstration of his wireless telegraph." Isn't that exciting?"

"Well, I ain't been sleeping, said 'Kitty Horatio' Let me tell you some of the stuff I heard." I still think that the architect got his plans mixed up when he built a fortress instead of a lighthouse. With the battlements along the roof and that mystery cannon they found, maybe, just maybe, he was preparing for an invasion rather than saving ships coming into the Harbor. And that 'first' new light everyone is talking about sure has not won any admiration awards. That beacon is so bright, all the residents are honked off 'cause they can't sleep, their cows won't give milk, and the chickens stopped laying eggs. But be careful what you ask for. That thing can be seen 22 miles out in the ocean. But the bigger the inspectors talked about is: Those lights might be the greatest thing since sliced bread, *but* if this new fangled 'perfect' apparatus for light-house lenses for the twin lights is rendered unfit - then what? If the Keepers have no clue how to fix it, you and I sure don't have a manual to help! Has anyone talked about a hidden room under the Keepers quarters. I could dig up a few more mysteries, I bet."

"Anything new, my brother, is going to have bumps along the way. The light has been fixed to not show so brightly over the residents, and look at two other wonderful 'firsts'. WE are going to have the *first* reading of the Pledge of Allegiance AND the first wireless transmission right here in our Navesink Twin Tower Lighthouse.

'Kitty Horatio' looked at his twin sister and smiled. "I'm thinkin' it's not only good to live in the Twin Tower lighthouse BUT be a twin brother to the smartest feline Lighthouse Keeper Mate around."

'Kitty Holly' smiled.

Chapter Six
What Are We Runnin' Here..a Barnyard or a Lighthouse!

"Good Mornin' 'Kitty Adiva', the always gleeful Esopus Meadows Lighthouse said to his friend. "Well, it would be a good morning if I didn't have to listen to that loud-mouthed rooster waking me up. I'm ready to put that bird in a pot for stew!"

"Now, now 'Kitty Adiva', remember we are still farm people. We have always lived in the green meadows. In fact, where we used to be right in the middle of the Hudson River, cows grazed at low tide. The Esopus Indians raised corn, squash and all sorts of berries and nuts here. 'Kitty Adiva' frowned, "All I'm sayin' is roosters crowing, two resident skunks runnin' amuck, cows mooing, and who knows how many cats and other critters. I am sure it makes people wonder if this is a barnyard or a lighthouse."

"Let me give you a little history about us. We aren't the first lighthouse built here. In 1831, Congress gave $3,000 to build a new lighthouse. The community kept waiting and waiting. After six years, costs went up, and the high tides created a need for a lighthouse to be built on a strong pier so the floating ice in the spring would not destroy everything. So, in 1837, Congress gave another $3,000 to construct the Esopus Meadows Lighthouse. Nothing fancy, just a 34 by 20 foot stone building topped by an octagonal tower and lantern room. Of course, placed on a nine-foot-high wooden pier. It had all the bells and whistles with four lamps and reflections in the Lantern room. Someone did not account, however, for the horrific flood tides and damaging ice flows. In fact, in 1869, the Keepers dwelling was deemed unfit to live in, and the pier needed to be taken away as well because of its condition. Having said that, she served her purpose. Mariners would be warned of the submerged mudflats plus be guided to safer waters to the east side of the river where they often faced many dangerous shallows."

'Kitty Adiva' listened quietly and then remarked, "So, all these animals have lived here for a long time. In fact, most grew up in the old lighthouse. I didn't come until the spring of 1871 when my parents were brought here as companions to the new Keepers in the newly rebuilt lighthouse. I was born here. "

"The story continues. In 1870 Congress once again gave $25,000 to rebuild me, but the money did not get here until too late to start construction. In the spring, the second lighthouse foundation began with 250 forty-foot-long poles that were driven into the river bed. Then, on top placed 12-inch square timbers and a circular granite pier. I think you would agree; we felt we were on solid footing. Now, here comes the interesting part. I am the only wood-frame lighthouse with a clapboard exterior on the river. Our fifth-order Fresnel lens is 58 feet above the river and was lit in August 1972. We lived here a long time before we opened for navigation. Our 2-story dwelling gave the Keepers a nice place to live. So you can see why the skunks run the rails of the lantern house, and 'Rocky', the rooster thinks he is in charge of the morning alarm. He does not seem to pay attention to the bell that strikes every ten seconds when needed. Since the Keepers station was only accessible from the water, 'Rocky' always went with his Keeper, Mr. Kern. He crows like a ship captain guiding the little boat to shore."

'Kitty Adiva' grinned. "Well, if it is okay with you, I will stay right here. People in town already think we are nuts living in a lighthouse that has roosters, skunks and a barnyard menagerie running wild. I am so glad this is my home. At least for now, we are all safe, well knowing some lighthouses have a short life."

One thing you might tell possible visitors, in the event they might want to visit the rebuilt *Esopus Meadows Lighthouse,* is whether the two skunks are deodarized or not!

Chapter Seven

"Dragon Rocks" - Where's the Dragon Slayer?

'Kitty Brojohn', named after the coastal Steamer, S.S Brother Jonathan, is lying outside the soon-to-be lit St. George Reef Lighthouse. "Hi 'Georgie', are you getting excited? It's been a long ten years for you, huh!" "You got that right! I remember early on how your Mama would ride the Steamer back and forth to the quarries two hundred round trip miles. She watched them cut the large slabs of granite that would hopefully keep me standing for years to come. I had to be strong enough to hold that huge First Order Fresnel lens seven stories high. I am what's called a wave-washed built lighthouse, which just means the ocean will hit me from all sides. They tell me I am the most expensive lighthouse ever built in America at $700,000+." "Well, in my opinion, if they didn't take so long to build you, they might have saved a little money", 'Kitty Brojohn' remarked. "I wonder if Sir Frances Drake and those other guys had a clue when they chose the "Dragon Rocks" located six miles off Point St. George. Good Grief. I know they must have been thinking about saving lives, but all the frigid waters, and gail winds, this is one inhospitable place!"

'Georgie' looked fondly at his newest feline Assistant Keeper. "You came from a long line of great feline Keepers, whether on ships or lighthouses. Before I was built here on the Point, incoming ships were being swallowed up at alarming frequency by all these dangerous rocks. Many, many maritime disasters were reported. I am being built because of the paddle Steamer, Brother Jonathan, with 244 passengers, and a crew with a shipment of gold that struck an uncharted rock and capsized. Only nineteen people survived. After his sinking in 1865, it got so much attention that Congress allocated more money than ever before to build me. With my beacon coming off North West Seal Rock, many ships, cargo and people will now be able to navigate to their destinations more safely, unlike the S.S Brother Jonathan." "My goodness, now I know why my mother named me 'Kitty Brojohn'. I will be the best Assistant Keeper I can be."

St. George Reef Lighthouse

First Light - 1892

Later

'Kitty Brojohn' yelled up to his friend, "Wow, wouldn't my parents love living here, 'Georgie'?"

"I think they would, but as you have come to know, these storms are fierce and intense. We aren't getting our much-needed supplies, and it is now not one of the most sought-after Keeper assignments. They can't get any relief lighthouse keepers because they can't get here. The Keepers are getting more and more stressed. Every time the glass is blown out in the lantern room, and a Keeper has to try and fix any damage, they put their lives on the line. Being a Keeper has to be one of the most important, dangerous and underpaid jobs in America."

"Well, ever since ole' Captain George Vancouver named the exposed and dangerous rocks off Point St. George - "Dragon Rocks", I have been waiting on that crazy "Dragon Slayer" to do his job!" frowned 'Kitty Brojohn'. "We need a break!"

His best friend, 'Georgie' laughed.

"Keep watching."

Chapter Eight
A Lighthouse Live-In School Teacher? Be careful. She Can be Tougher Than Wet Leather!

"Children, this is Agatha McNeary, your new live-in school teacher." 'Kitty Rondo' opened one eye from his usual mid-morning nap and said to his lighthouse buddy, "Hey 'Ripley', How long will it take her to get out of that *uniform*? I hear they have a bunch of dumb rules. One, they have to wear two petticoats. Another, her hair has to be piled on top of her head, and she can't be married. White blouse -long black skirt. Gracious me. No wonder she ain't married. She looks like she eats nails for breakfast in that get-up. I'll count how many trips up and down that spiral staircase until she takes a roll. Then the misses will tell her to take those silly petticoats off. Ain't no petticoat police roamin' around this isolated place anyway."

"I do believe it is going to be quite a change since she has to teach two girls and two boys. Mr. & Mrs. Lordes, my Keepers, want the boys to learn how to be inventive and enterprising. The biggest need out there is engineers, politicians and ministers. The girls...well, perhaps good wives, cooks, housekeepers or teachers. Mr. Lordes doesn't have much interest in that discussion. His thinking is to teach them to read and write..you know basics."

Lighthouse 'Ripley' said, "I heard them going over Miss

McNeary's resume and her credentials/recommendation letters. Her contract said she was also to teach about lighthouses since the children have had no experience in living and working in a lighthouse. She passed with flying colors and the Teacher Code Agreement as well. The standard uniform, never show your ankles, no drinking of spirits, no chewing, and keeping no male company." 'Kitty Rondo' cracked up. "Wondering where they think a male might come calling? He better know how to swim or row a boat!!"

Miss Agatha met the children and told them her lesson plans for them. Most days, it would be the same, but she had some surprises for what they would do differently, especially when the weather permits. Boys and girls would be separated except at the 8:00 am hour. "I will read a short scripture daily, followed by prayer and singing. We will learn some hymnal and patriotic songs, and at certain holiday times, we will sing songs appropriate to the season. You will be neatly dressed, hair combed and your daily primers with you each day, and of course, your homework assignments completed. Any questions?

Twelve-year-old Charlie spoke up. "Mama said you know how to make taffy!!" "Well, we will have to see about that closer to Christmas. Only children who do their lessons and behave in class are rewarded. You might want to remember that."

Miss McNeary looked over at 'Kitty Rondo' and smiled, "Welcome to our class. From time to time, I know you will be great in helping me teach the children about ships and lighthouses." "Okay, 'Ripley,' did you put her up to that?" 'Ripley' replied, "You might learn something."

"Good morning, children", said Miss McCleary. "Good Morning, teacher." "Today is Monday. I would like to go over our weekly assignments. Girls, you will see on your table a round wooden 'hoop', a piece of cloth that has a needle in the center. On that cloth is a group of "x's" that will spell the word MONDAY. Each day, we will work on a different day of the week until seven days/dish towels are completed. This might make your mother a nice Christmas gift. Now, you can go to your table and open your primer to Chapter One. I will join you shortly. Boys, we will start our journey learning about your home, the lighthouse. Today, you will see on your table a list of questions about the Fresnel Lens. By the end of the week, you will know all about the beacon that guides ships so they won't crash into our shore. On your table, you will see a small wooden chalkboard with a small eraser. *Do Not throw your eraser or abuse the chalk!* If you do, punishment will be swift." "Teacher, Father was worried because he thought your big steamer trunk might sink the ship you came in on", giggled Jester. "That trunk has many teaching treasures that you will see along the way. It's like building this lighthouse. You need lots of tools, Jester. Now, to start, let's open your primers, and we will read chapter one together." She then put on her tiny spectacles that rested on her nose most of the time. The school year began in earnest.

During the next few months, the girls finished their sewing projects with pride and the importance of housekeeping in a lighthouse. Especially the right way to clean the tower glass. The boys not only learned about the workings of a lighthouse but a greater understanding of the Keeper and Assistant Keepers jobs. One slip-up could cost hundreds of lives and precious cargo to be lost at sea. They planted an indoor garden, learned quilting out of material scraps, and could recite the Pledge of Allegiance and sing Amazing Grace. The boys were heard talking to 'Kitty Rondo' about becoming Lighthouse Keepers.

Miss Agatha McNeal 'earned her stripes', but was known as one of the most creative, intelligent and patient lighthouse teachers of her time. Many remote lighthouses adopted the live-in schoolhouse teacher as a preferred method of teaching for their children, thanks to her success.

Miss McNeal surprised her four special students with homemade taffy individually wrapped as their Christmas reward.

'Kitty Rondo' and Lighthouse 'Ripley' smiled.

Chapter Nine
Get Away From My Lighthouse, Or I'll Show You What a Real Army Is!

"Our Ship Island Lighthouse, even though delayed in its construction, still has the multiple lamp and reflector system upgrade fourth-order Fresnel lens. People fighting over who owned the land took forever to get it all worked out", said 'Kitty Wackle' to his friend, 'Kitty Pooli'. "The Mississippi Sand is known for its shallow, dark waters and is a treacherous area for vessels navigating between Mobile and New Orleans. And don't forget the hurricanes and resulting shifting sands that also create havoc. Because of all the commercial shipping traffic, we really needed the government's help in getting us a lighthouse", remarked 'Kitty Pooli'.

"'Kitty Pooli', What are you hearing about the Civil War?", "Not good. Very frightening, and I don't know what's going to happen!" "Do you think we should hold a meeting of the Ship Cats and the entire Defense Warriors?" "I believe if the Confederate forces try to take our Island, we should be prepared."

'Kitty Wackle', Ship Cat of the U.S. Flusser, served with his Master and Commander in the U.S. Naval forces in Europe, and 'Kitty Pooli', who was born in a naval yard and survived several Second World War battles called the largest contingent of Defense Warriors on the island to discuss the secret Operation 'RatFink'.

The Confederate army seized the little island at the beginning of the Civil War, but when they decided to take over the lighthouse and set fire to her, Operation 'RatFink' jumped into action. "Batallion Wheat Sacks", 200 mice strong, tore into every feed sack, the supply depot of flour, sugar, and any supplies that fed the army personnel on the island. 150 Rat Patrol charged quietly throughout the entire barracks to include tents, and the horse stables. They successfully chewed every rope and any form of communication and even included all the horse ropes used to tie up the horses. Another two hundred assorted rodents harassed the sleeping soldiers by racing all over the place, including their beds, and leaving a few bites that gave every soldier sleepless nights. At a specific time, all patrols were expected to return to their usual places of 'employment' and not be seen by a soul.

'Kitty' Wackle and 'Kitty' Pooli gave each other a high-fi for a job well executed. "Our Commanders would be proud." "The Confederate forces may have stolen our beloved lighthouse lens and set it on fire, but the Union forces are coming, and there is no need for Operation 'Rat Fink'. I have been told by my connections that they will restore our Ship Island Lighthouse to operation with a new lens and lantern. It will be different than the one stolen, and the light will be blocked out to the North to prevent its use by any blockade runners that might approach the mainland."

As reported, the Union Forces did start to restore our lighthouse, but a General in charge remarked. "We have been here for weeks, and there are two cats who seem to know this lighthouse and the island in and out, but it was reported that there were thousands of mice and rats that ate or tore up everything in sight. Know anything about that? We have not seen one RAT or MOUSE on this island since we got here."

"Sir, I am thinking those Confederate runners rarely tell the truth."

Ship Island Lighthouse in Mississippi may have, over time, lost her battle with hurricane abuse, a leaning tower that collapsed and survived numerous restorations, but there has *never* been a report that Ship Cats Operation 'Rat Fink' ever activated the Defense Warriors again.

No doubt people would think it just too good to be true!

'Kitty Wackle' and 'Kitty Pooli' retired shortly after the Ship Island Lighthouse renovation.

Chapter Ten
I Told Mother We Are Going to be Living in a Lighthouse. She Fainted!

"Arthur, Arthur, come here immediately!" a hysterical Mrs. Arthur Martini screamed. "She's gone, she eloped with John, and she took 'Kitty Peebles' with her! Edith, bring that letter she left on the hall table and bring my smelling salts. I feel faint."

A Letter to Father and Mother

"I know this is very difficult for you and equally difficult for us. Mother, I know that you had made many plans for me to attend the Teachers College and beyond, and will be deeply disappointed. John has been in the Lighthouse Service for three years and is now to be promoted to Head Lighthouse Keeper. They want him to report to the Point Bonita Lighthouse located at the San Francisco Bay entrance. We were married this morning before boarding the train. I promise to start immediately by sending you a journal of our days in the new lighthouse. Be happy for me.

Lovingly, your daughter, Jenna.

Ruby Martini openly declared her life was ruined, and the Ladies of the VERY private social club would be horrified that her daughter did not attend the Teachers College nor get properly married in the church. Arthur was less emotional. "I need to go to work." Ruby had to be taken to her bed. The duration was not determined.

Jenna's Journal was full even before arriving in California. She wrote: "The gold rush has certainly changed many lives. Numerous ships coming and going to service the huge migration of people and the needed supplies for extracting gold have created a dangerous setting for sure. All of this has created a need for a Lighthouse. Congress allocated twenty-five thousand dollars for Point Bonita, and I know John will make a great contribution.

We were met with numerous surprises. Intense fog that never lets up, dangerous shoals that make it very difficult for ships, and currents that have been responsible for so many loss of lives. Over 300 boats have run aground near the Golden Gate. Lighthouse Keepers are continually pulling people out of the water before they perish. Many never make it safely to shore."

"Today, we realized the Lighthouse Tower can only be reached by a narrow wooden footbridge. And the Tower itself sits horribly close to a narrow ledge overlooking the Golden Gate. 'Kitty Peebles' has her own opinions. She commented to her new lighthouse friend, 'Bony', she calls him, " Someone sure didn't know what they were doing when they picked this site and built a lighthouse that had a 56 ft brick tower, 306 feet above sea level with Fresnel lens. Because guess what! It was too high! The California fog leaves lower elevations clear, and no ship can see the light through the fog. What were they thinking? Now, they have to do some creative navigational aids, or we won't be needed here."

Jenna wrote a short note to her parents. "We are in the process of moving to a lower location. 124 ft above sea level. John is helping oversee a 118-foot tunnel that is being hand-carved through very hard rock. 'Kitty Pebbles' seems to be enjoying all the constant activity with the building of our new cottage to include a fireplace. Think we know where her favorite spot will be. More later, Jenna."

Later, Jenna wrote: "Sorry it has been so long in between writings. My journal always seems to be hidden under something with all that is going on. So often, we are shrouded in fog, and the new navigational aid, an 8-foot-long cannon, will soon be operational. Thankfully, John won't be responsible for firing it once every half hour in times of fog. Someone else has been hired to do that. They are working on a steam fog siren, but our landslides are creating havoc in finding a more secure place for a fog signal. These are exciting times. I will try to write more often. Lovingly, Jenna and 'Kitty Pebbles'

Jenna wrote, "I have to tell you a funny, but not so funny happening. Our Assistant Keeper and his lovely wife have two children. When they go out to play, it is mandatory that they are strapped into a rope harness. Since the Tower sits precariously on a narrow ledge, it is not hard to see why. Well, the other week, little Georgie was not readily seen. Everybody rushed out, and Georgie was seen danging over the ledge. "His mother wants a transfer!" 'Kitty Pebbles' said. We were to get no ideas about putting one of those apparatuses on him. His friend, 'Kitty Kasey' is tethered all the time, and he declares a big No Way!

"The weeks, months and years seem to go by quickly. We have just been told that the Chinese workmen responsible for the Sierra tunnels of the Transcontinental Railroad are coming to dig a 118-foot tunnel through the mountain rock. The tunnel will allow the railway to be extended from the loading platform to the fog signal and the area where we reside. Never a dull moment in the United States Lighthouse Service. I am helping anywhere I can, and 'Kitty Pebbles', John and I are always ready for a cup of hot tea at day's end. The waves breaking around the rocks and the gorgeous sunset makes us proud to know we are truly guardians of the Northern tip of the Golden Gate. "

Mrs. Ruby Martini proudly reported that her son-in-law, John Brown, had been awarded The Golden Headed Cane by the Office of Collector of Customs for his Lighthouse service. Over 40 lives had been saved by his heroic efforts while serving as the Lighthouse Keeper at Point Bonita. Seems her fainting spells were a thing of the past. Although her daughter, Jenna, never became a teacher, she was given the Assistant Keepers position and became one of the first women to reach that level. Arthur and Ruby also received word later that year they were to be grandparents. Now, Ruby really had something to worry about. She is already at work making a very strong harness.

John, Jenna and 'Kitty Pebbles' served in the Lighthouse service for over thirty years and raised their family there.

Chapter Eleven
Split Rock Lighthouse? Does that Mean Half Goes On One Side and Half on the Other?

'Kitty Apelsin,' named after a most beautiful orange sunset seen at the end of each day on The Lakes. Her wide orange stripes that go all the way to the end of her tail and eyes that mirror the ocean's blue-green color make her quite a standout as she strolls through the once-called 'construction site'. "What a remote and barren-looking place this was. With the cutting of the trees down the cliff for the much-needed Lighthouse, a pack of wolves couldn't make as much noise as the wind that howled loud and large." she said to her friend 'Kitty Tinker', the mascot and companion to the l

Lighthouse engineer.

"He sure had his work cut out for him, said 'Kitty Tinker'. Lake Superior and the inhospitable North Shore have no land access except by water. Before you got here, supplies by boats were few and far between. Adding to that, the l

Lighthouse was far from any supply depot."

'Kitty Apelsin' said, "We both know how we came to be here. The shipwrecks were the worst in 1905. Everybody says they were unlike any seen before in our time. That November gale took out at least 30 ships, including four vessels of the Pittsburgh Steamship Company. Hundreds of thousands of dollars were lost, and many lives as well. Soon after that horrific event, the President of the Pittsburgh Steamship Company led a whole delegation to Washington, D.C., urging the U.S Lighthouse Service to construct a lighthouse. It took a while, but Congress giving $75,000 sure helped. Not only to get us a lighthouse but a fog signal on 7.6 acres at Split Rock."

"Yes, I remember well. The storm on Minnesota's north shore barreled down and broke everything in sight, and numerous vessels just disappeared, never to be seen again. The blizzard blinded all vessels and could not get warnings that had gone out trying to warn all ships that were in the sea to get to shore fast. Many freighters carrying freshly mined ore from Minnesota's Iron Range and many others did not escape the Mataafa Blow Storm and perished. That is how Mr. Tinkham and I ended up in Split Rock. He, as the lighthouse engineer, and I, as his companion."

'Kitty Tinker', "We are so fortunate to have met and get to live here. We have great Keepers, and I love hearing the children play near their houses. So many things have happened since we arrived, including the installation of a beautiful beacon that now makes the tower rise to 168 feet above sea level and has a range of 22 miles. Now that saves lives!! "

"What a journey, 'Kitty Apelsin'. We did not realize how hard it would be to design and construct the Split Rock Light Station. No road to the site, and workers and building supplies had to be shipped by boat. Think about hoisting tons of brick and other materials up a 130-foot rock cliff by a steam-powered derrick.

Unpredictable wind often brought everything to a halt. But, I have to tell you, this magnificent, octagonal yellow brick lighthouse that now sits high up on a jaggedy cliff is, without a doubt, one of the most picturesque sites to behold. Mr. Tinkham is a fabulous engineer", 'Kitty Tinker' proudly boasted.

"Want to know a secret? 'Kitty Tinker' asked, laughing out loud." "What?" 'Kitty Apelsin,' replied. "Do you know the best part was when that construction contractor hired a REAL French Chef to cook for all of us? The workers weren't the only ones who were kept happy on the project!"

The two friends chuckled and walked over to watch the children play.

Chapter Twelve
What Do You Do? I Save Lives on Pea Island!

"Richard Etheridge and 'Kitty Krewler' reporting for duty, SIR! We are joining the 36th United States Colored Group of the United States Life-Saving Service, SIR!"

"What might your qualifications be?" asked General Ambrose Burnside. "Sir, my name is Richard Etheridge, and this is 'Kitty Krewler'. I was born a slave on the outer banks of North Carolina. My Master taught me to work the sea, how to pilot boats, how to fish to live, and how to comb the beaches for shipwreck debris. He also taught me to read and write, SIR" 'Kitty Krewler' was born on a slave ship and knows all the ins and outs of the importance of ship safety. He and his crew are responsible for helping to save many lives who might have been lost at sea."

"You will be assigned to the Pea Island U.S Life-Saving Station in the outer banks of North Carolina. You will be part of the first all-black crew and have a black Commander. We finally got the attention of Congress after many efforts by private and humanitarian groups showed the great need to save the lives of shipwrecked mariners and passengers. We need you and your crew to help provide life-saving service, as well as assist the Lighthouse Keepers in various tasks. Your jobs are not quite 24 hours a day, *but* ships can wreck at any time, and you will need to be prepared." "Yes, SIR."

Later, During the American Civil War. A Day in the Life of a Life-Saving Station.

'Kitty Krewler' seemed to have a keen sense of the changing weather on Pea Island and remarked that the seas were very quickly changing that day. "What is that? Looks like the schooner E.L Newman, but the hurricane winds and high squalls are forcing her into the jagged rocks. I know that the Captain always travels this route with his wife and daughter. I feel we need to get the mule team out and have the beach cart with our rescue equipment and surfboat ready. This does not look good." Richard Etheridge agreed and mobilized the crew and all of a sudden, the dim lights indicating trouble at sea began to fade. " All the best swimmers NOW!! Theodore, tether yourself, and I will do the same. Others, you know your jobs..now let's execute all that training."

"Richard shouted, "There is nothing going to work except swimming to the schooner and heaving a line aboard before she sinks. Let's go! Theodore made nine trips, and due to the efforts of the first Pea Island Life-Saving Station all-black crew, every passenger and crew member was rescued. 'Kitty Krewler' was anxiously waiting on the little girl to get on shore. His shiny black fur was much like a beacon with dancing big black eyes. He saw her immediately. She was shaking and was quickly wrapped in a thick blanket. Warm milk was on its way. When 'Kitty Krewler' climbed on top of her blanket, she stopped crying and dozed off to sleep. "You see, we all have our jobs to do."

There seemed to be little time for awards for heroic duty, but a wooden sideboard with the name E.C. Newman was found floating to shore and was given to Theodore Meekins for his service. Entire crew clapped and then back to work as usual. It appeared an arsonist had burned the Life-Saving Station to the ground. Many refused to accept an all-black crew and made no mention of their life-saving heroism. They rebuilt the station with pride and added quarters for those who were temporarily displaced by a shipwreck. That was not in anyone's job description.

On August 2, 2012, the second Coast Guard's 154-foot Sentinal Class Cutters, USCGC Richard Etheridge (WPC-1102), was commissioned in his honor. The first black Commanding Officer of U.S. Life-Saving Service.

Chapter Thirteen

Woman Keepers are the Best. They Know How to Clean the Lens.

'Kitty Blanco', named after her newly built lighthouse, commented that after they had cleared all the spruce from the land on the Cape, there was enough wood piled up to heat three winter fireplaces. "I can remember when I went back and forth to the local craftsman shops while they were making 200,000 brick for your tower and duplex, and all of a sudden, a huge gale struck about when they were unloading the vessel and drove that ship right into the beach! I thought we would never get you built." 'Capey' said, " I was so thrilled when my light came on right before Christmas, and you were able to issue the new year in with me. We can now warn ships away from these nasty reefs."

Mr. & Mrs. Bretherton have done some serious Keeper jobs here on the Oregon coast. Mabel Bretherton had worked alongside her husband and was quite proficient at knowing how to keep light and lens perfect for any possible ship that might show up at sea in need of help. She always said that the job was the most important one that a Keeper had to do. 'Kitty Blanco' said, "Unfortunately, Mr. Bretherton was losing his battle with tuberculosis and passed away, leaving Miss Mabel and her three children behind."

"We are so fortunate, 'Capey' remarked. That Mabel Bretherton got *her first* lighthouse job with us." 'Kitty Blanco', "Did you know that The Lighthouse Service offers employment and housing to a Keepers widow and children? Because she had worked at two other Lighthouses, she was a great candidate for us." 'Kitty Blanco" laughed out loud. "And you know what else? She is the *first Oregon* woman lighthouse Keeper." "I am so excited to have three little ones running around. They are all under the age of ten, and I can help a lot. Especially when those storms are running amuck, and Miss Mabel is needed up top. "

"How are we doing, 'Capey? Miss Mabel asked after a really horrific storm. "Well, we are the highest Oregon lighthouse above sea level at 245 ft., and our lights are performing perfectly. Your work taking care of the light and lens from dusk to dawn is certainly saving lives. Teasingly, he added. "But somehow, we need to figure out how we can teach 'Kitty Blanco' how to clean and polish the glass during the daylight hours."

'Kitty Blanco' pretended to be tending to three little boys.

Chapter Fourteen

How Do I Find Love in a Lighthouse?

Just Court a Girl by Semaphore!

'Kitty Valentia' saw Ellen Bartlet standing at the edge of the sea waving her hands. " I best go down and see what she is up to before her father has another fit. Her holiday summer vacation from nursing college has not really gone well. Seems Charles Harwood III became smitten with Ellen when he was a relief lighthouse keeper. He knew she loved flowers and planting vegetables, so he brought barrels of dirt and packets of seeds so she could have a real 'rock garden'. Her father had no objections about that since it helped feed their large family. But, it stopped there."

"Hey, 'Halpi',' Kitty Valentia' yelled at his lighthouse friend. I'm gonna go check on Ellen." 'Halpi' quickly replied, "You better get prepared for an explosion, but not a ship hitting rocks. It will be her father when he finds out she is sending messages back and forth to Charles by semaphore 800 yards across the water. She is not waving her hands - she is waving flags. Also, be prepared for the carrier pigeon whom they are teaching to transport messages. They soon became known as the Maiden Lovers. Ellen is strong-minded, and her father may have met his match."

The cottage-style lighthouse has an open coal fire in a 'roof-top brazier.' Even though coal is used, leftover oakum is also used, as well as candles. 'Halpi reminded 'Kitty Valentia' that all the large families, like our Keeper, who live in the lighthouse year-round, must have strong, able-bodied assistants to help make sure the bonfire does not go out and the metal baskets are tended. Running up and down stairs wears any person out after a while. Unfortunately, the Bartlets had more girls than boys, and most were not being groomed to be lighthouse keepers. Consequently, many relief keepers hired to assist were young men who often fell in love with the lighthouse keepers' daughters. That worked out well for Ellen and Charles until a fallout over the romance that occurred between the two families. It was thought that the romance got shut down before it had a chance to blossom or not!

Mrs. Bartlet looked at 'Kitty Valencia' and shared her frustration. "We have eleven children to feed. Here, it is nearly Thanksgiving, and no supplies have reached us in weeks. Our Thanksgiving dinner, as it stands now, consists of boiled potatoes and bread. I don't know what to do!" 'Kitty Valencia' knew there was a storm brewing because 'Halpi' told him the lanterns needed to be as bright as they could be.

Later that day. Lighthouse 'Halpi' shouted to 'Kitty Valencia', "Hurry up here now!! Look outside the lantern window. Three ducks were attracted to the light and ran into the lantern. Hurry, go get Mrs. Bartlet and the girls. Thanksgiving dinner just got better." One could say, all present around the table had a 'Ducky' dinner - even with some trimmings.

Shortly after Thanksgiving, Ellens' father found out about the romantic use of the Semaphore visual signaling. We are told not just Charles could read the blossoming romance signaling between two young lovers coming from the Maidens Lighthouse. *Swiftly,* she was sent back to Dublin to finish her nursing studies. However, Charles did not give up. Not even!

Charles and Ellen eloped and were married after her nursing school graduation. They returned to the stunning landscapes and the romantic towers of light and love. Both served in The Lighthouse Service for three decades.

We have it from good authority, the Commissioner of Irish Lights, that this is not an Irish fable.

Chapter Fifteen

Grandpa, Tell Us The Story Again About Old Bark Shanty

'Kitty Barky' snuggled up to his friend Roscoe, a third-generation Lighthouse Keeper, close to the warmth of the burning fireplace. The forecast was the typical fierce winds and fog so thick you could cut it with a knife. It made for a perfect day for telling the grandchildren the stories they had heard many times before, and staying inside.

As you know, your great, great grandfather, Roscoe Wilhelm I, was a lumberman. He, along with many others, came to pull bark from the Hemlock trees. Many of the men were tanners. "What is a tanner, Grandpa?" "It is a person who uses tree bark to scrape animal hides so you can make clothing, boots and bags that won't easily get wet. So, when many men were there working, they would build what they called a 'bark shanty'. Wasn't much to look at. More of a lean-to to get protection from the beastly weather. More important was the huge fire the lumbermen built and kept burning all the time. Because it was visible from the lake, the Shanty became a great landmark to sailors on Lake Huron. That's how it got its name, Bark Shanty Point."

'Kitty Barky' looked at his best friend, lighthouse 'Porty', a name he gave him when the town renamed Bark Shanty Point to Lighthouse Port Sanilac, and said, "We are gonna get to the good part soon." 'Porty' said, "I can only imagine what he will tell this time. You know he changes it every time he tells the story."

"What happened next, Grandpa?" Well, when they built the shipping docks into the lake, it no longer was a lumberjack settlement. Things really started changing. Problem was that

Congress didn't want to give the necessary money to build lighthouses to provide the necessary lights so vessels could navigate safely from the foot of the lake around the tip of Michigan's "thumb". "Thumb"? What was that? It was a 75-mile stretch that remained unlighted. Vessel Masters were running 'totally in the dark' along a forty-mile stretch of coastline with no visibility from either of the two lights to help them navigate away from rocks and dangerous waters. Your great-grandfather, Roscoe II, was very frustrated. He told about two steamers being stuck on the ice and all of the St. Claire River was blocked." An attentive grandson, Carl said, "I bet that got some people's attention!"

'Kitty Barky' mumbled and yawned, "'Kitty Porty', tell him that's enough history. Get to the good part." "Grandpa, tell us about the logbook you had to keep."

Everyone got quiet. 'Porty' was watching the sea but listening. 'Kitty Barky' stood up, shook his thick winter coat and repositioned himself nearer the fire. "Well, I came on board just as they mandated all Keepers had to keep daily log books. At the end of each watch, I had to write every little thing that happened. I preferred the 'watching' part to the 'writing' part'. Who cares about the daily duties of a lighthouse Keeper? There are only so many boring navigation issues, drills and exercises, ceremonies, official visits and personnel things to write about.

Then Grandpa Roscoe III said, "I do have to say it wasn't all bad. We got real good at writing love notes to the ladies who worked in the lighthouses as assistants." "Is that where you met Grandmother?" "I think you know that was the best part of keeping logs. Sometimes, no one noticed or cared what the temperature was, or the names of the incoming or outgoing vessels were. So, we could slip things between the lines.

And I actually proposed to your grandmother in a log!! "

"Did she accept?"

"She sure did! We had all four of your parents in this Lighthouse!!" And, the very best part is what?" All the children shouted, "We were born here too!!"

'Kitty Barky' and 'Porty' smiled. No matter the middle of the story, the ending is always the same!